HOW TO BE GREATEST AT ORAL SEX:

SEX SECRETS THAT PUTS A SPELL ON HIM

Special Edition

By:

Jessica King

HOW TO BECOME THE GREATEST AT ORAL SEX:

SEX SECRETS THAT PUTS A SPELL ON HIM

Special Edition

Published on Amazon.com in 2014 by Jessica King

Copyright © 2014 by Jessica King

This book and the power it contains
are dedicated to you . . .

Acknowledgements

My fans from around the world, thank you for your unwavering support.

My publicists, Ana, thanks girl! You have made my career this huge success, thank you.

My entire team and my friends and my family, I love you all so much, thank you.

To everyone who chooses to read this book to see what it's about, thank you such much for the opportunity. My heart goes out to you.

"Books are a uniquely portable magic."
— **Stephen King**, *On Writing: A Memoir of the Craft*

"And above all, watch with glittering eyes the whole world around you because the greatest secrets are always hidden in the most unlikely places. Those who don't believe in magic will never find it."

— **Roald Dahl**

"Magic is believing in yourself, if you can do that, you can make anything happen."
— **Johann Wolfgang von Goethe**

FOREWARD

This book is enlightenment. It sheds light on an age of practice that has always been shrouded in mystery. The spirit inside me prompted me to write it so that women can become free and enlightened and become more aware of the infinite power within them.

CONTENTS

1. The Intangible Power of Thought
2. The Emotion of Desire
3. The Magic Power of Believing
4. The Magical Spells of Affirmations
5. The Magical Emotion of Love
6. Feminine Rebirth
7. The Magic of Sexual Energy
8. The Ancient Art of Transmutation

9. The Art of Oral Sex part 1:Foreplay
10. The Art of Oral Sex Part 2: The Act
11. How to place a sexual spell on a guy (Bonus Chapter)
12. How to make him to stick to you sexually (Bonus Chapter)

Chapter 1:

The Intangible Power of Thought

You have taken the first step towards power, power that will aid you in becoming the greatest at oral sex, power that will leave him in a trance, power that will put a spell on him. The starting point herein is the power of your thinking or in simple terms the power of your *thoughts*.

Did you know that what you think about you bring about? Yes, thoughts persisted in will manifest into your life, therefore, with persistence and controlled attention you can develop your latent powers. The *Key* is your thoughts.

Thoughts can be either negative or positive, there is no in-between. Therefore, if your thoughts are not positive then they are negative and the thoughts you need to develop your latent power are *positive* thoughts.

To change anything or to accomplish anything you must first learn to control yourself and your thinking.

Thoughts are things and they are powerful things. If you doubt my statement, pause and take a look around you now, every object, item, merchandise, electronic etc, that is around you now was first conceived as a thought in the human mind. Thoughts are things and powerful things at that.

How can you use thoughts to become the greatest at oral sex? It is simple, train yourself to think that you are the greatest, becoming greater, and your skills are increasing everyday.

Thoughts have their impact on the mind which operates on the conscious and subconscious level, if you are able to use your thoughts to convince yourself then it will awaken then infinite power within you.

Chapter 2:

The Emotion of Desire

Desire is a very powerful form of energy. Thoughts are forms of energy and they become alive when mixed with desire, its thoughts that are mixed with feelings and emotions that impacts our mind the most and leaves a deeper imprint.

If you truly want to place a spell on a guy then began at once to work on your desire. We are women and our needs are vast, it is time we wake up and rise up and realize the infinite power within us. Desire is the need or want for someone or something, its one of the most powerful form of positive emotion. The more you persist in a thought the stronger your desire becomes so begin at once to think about that guy whom you wish to sweep off his feet. Feel the intense burning within your heart, feel the tingle in the top of your head, feel the butterflies in your stomach when you think about him, learn to feel this emotion deeply, the more you can feel it the more you can practice control of it and *call upon it at will* when the times comes.

Visualize his face, picture him naked, imagine yourself before him, hear him moan your name as pleasures sweep him away, do this and feel the intense desire building up inside you. This is raw power and the more you practice the more powerful you will become. Practice this carefully for you will need it when the time comes, I know you have been feeling it all your life but this time you are for the first time becoming consciously aware that it is a form of power, energy and magic that will be put to aid for you.

Practice becomes *perfect*.

Chapter 3:

The Magic Power of Believing

Let us hereby look at the third form of *magic* that you will need in this endeavor, it's called the magic of believing. Everything that you have ever wanted to happen to or for you that has happened; happened because you tapped into the universal law of believing.

Belief moulds and creates your reality and the world around you. Whatever the human mind can conceive and believe the human mind can achieve. Belief is the foundation of all religions, we walk by faith and not by sight, you and every other person around you ought to be interested in this magic power of believing that can and always have worked wonders in your life.

When you create thoughts that you will be the greatest at oral sex and you will blow that guys mind, and you mix desire with those thoughts, go ahead a step further, in faith, and place *belief* behind it. This will work miracles.

You must keep doing this, it might take you hours, days, weeks, months or years but it all depends on you. How many barriers you have placed around your mind? How sceptic are you? Rip these barriers down and approach this from an open minded perspective, closed minds do not inspire faith or believe or make room for it. Open up your heart, mind and soul and give it over to powers stronger than you if you wish to obtain this power, it has always been inside you . . . waiting for you to claim it.

Day in and day out you must believe in yourself, develop self-confidence. Write down a self-confidence formula that will aid you tremendously. Write down positive statements about yourself, with stronger self-confidence you tap into the power of belief for you begin to feel better about yourself once you believe it. In the chapter that follows will be a formula you can use to tap into this power.

Chapter 4:

The Magical Spells of Affirmations

Affirmations are repeated words, orders or self-suggestions; they are powerful and empowering statements for the sole purpose that they impact your mind through constant repetition. These are the known source of development of the power of faith. Repeated statements eventually cross over and are absorbed by your subconscious mind, the source of infinite power within you! This portion of your mind will transform you into *whatever* you desire to be.

Do you want to become the *greatest at oral sex?* Then this instruction must be given to your subconscious mind and you can do this by means of repeated words called affirmations that you imbued with emotions. Plain and meaningless words do not impress the subconscious mind; it understands and responds to the language of emotion.

Below is a short list of affirmative phrases you can begin to use immediately. However, the best time for affirmations is before you go to sleep at night, or as you wake during the morning.

Remember you are reading this book for the sole purpose of perfecting an age old art, and though these methods may seem abstract; do them anyways if you want power!

I Am the greatest at oral sex.

I leave guys weak when I perform oral sex on them.

I Am very powerful.

My infinite powers are awaking now, I can feel it, I believe it.

(Insert the guy name here that you wish to place a spell on)_____ loves when I give him oral sex, it leaves him weak and breathless.

(Insert the guy name here that you wish to place a spell on)_____ is falling in love with me because my oral sex skills blows his mind.

I have faith in myself and in my own abilities.

I Am proud of myself, I am getting better at oral sex day by day.

I Am a master of oral sex.
My oral sex skills are unmatched, I Am the Best.

I Am happy and thankful now that I Am the Greatest at Oral Sex.

I Am so thankful that my oral sex skills leaves guys weak in their knees.

I Am so happy and thankful that my Oral Sex skills puts sexual spells on guys.

I Am thankful that guys loves me, my oral sex skills blows their minds.

These statements are actual spells only if you attached feelings and emotions to them along with faith that they will work, if you do not, and expect no change or no difference in your condition then certainly you will get whatever you expect. Clear your mind of doubt and fear and they will work! You will become powerful!

Chapter 5:

The Magical Emotion of Love

This is by far the most powerful form of positive emotions. When you attached this to any thought with faith, it manifest faster.

If you would like your spells to work faster then attach an intense burning feeling of love with them. If you want a guy to fall in love with you, then visualize what its like when both of you are in love, use your imagination to picture going out, making memories together and making love, imagine him saying nice things to you and act in this spirit everyday, act how you would act when you are in love.

The power of love never fails, love comes when it pleases and goes away without warning, spend no time worrying about it because worry will never bring it back. Love is spiritual in nature and leaves a deep imprint upon the human heart, if you truly desire love, then fall in love with yourself and imagine being in love with the person, create affirmations of them falling in love with you. There is a power that will do the rest, *just believe* . . .

Chapter 6:

Feminine Rebirth

All that you need to know about the power you need is inside you, please allow your brain cells to click into being without your rational conscious mind trying to define everything to the minutest detail. *Act in faith*, with the power of your *desires* and *love* and *act now*.

Who is it that you would like to place the spell on? You decide and lay the path for him to follow. Make him feel more than lust for you, do something nice for him to trigger the emotions of *love, gratitude* and *appreciation* inside him for you. If his birthday is near, do something nice for him; avoid sexual activities until you have completed this little manual for upon completion, the new you will be born. Buy him something nice or offer money if you have it, do whatever little you can so that it will be *appreciated*, laying the foundation for the next step.

Let him see you as you are now, the person he has always seen, just as ordinary as you are. Smile and feel good within yourself for you know that big changes are underway!

The Caterpillar

Imagine yourself as you are now, knowing nothing and is an ordinary human being. Work on your *thoughts*, *affirmations*, *desires* and feeling of *love* and *faith*. Practice day and night, day and night and know that you are becoming powerful day by day!

The Cocoon

Are you ready for change? Or you wish to remain as you are? You can choose power, it as always been available to all who are ready for it, are you? Will you make the change now or wait and remain as you are?

Do you want to play with *magic beyond your wildest imagination . . .*?

Get on your knees and pray for powers beyond imagining and believe this is being given to you. Ask for the power to evolve into the goddess you were meant to be.

Work on your powers and persist with faith!

The Butterfly, the Goddess within you

Ok women, let's get the show rolling.

Do something to your hair, make a change, this can be coloring it, cutting it, straightening it or curling, do what makes you feel comfortable and sexy. Sexy is the target and if you already always felt sexy its time to up the game!

Get a pedicure and manicure! Change the color of your nails, if red or pink is fine with you then go for it, red raises your sexual energy so go for more red.

Wear nice pants, shirts, blouse, nice shoes, nice heels, wedge heels!

Shop! It does not matter if your clothing is not expensive; the goal here is to look and feel comfortable in them. Radiate self-confidence with your thoughts!

Try new makeup, go for a fierce look!

Look, walk, talk and act in confidence. People will notice a change, men will gravitate towards you! Nothing is wrong with wanting to be wanted; the feeling is natural and inborn and should not be suppressed because of what other people say. Ignore people and their trashy talk, you are moving forward and the attention is on you. Maintain a positive personality and deal with people in a nice and friendly manner, they will literally fall before your feet and worship you! Everyone loves a sweetheart and one who is nice and friendly with the bonus of dangerously sexy will have the world behind her. Treat nicely even those who hate and persecute you, remember the power of love, faith and desire are your friends now, these energy radiate within you and are yours to get whatever you desire.

Wear sexy clothing, sexy bra, and shop for new g-string and lingerie, ignore size, get what fits you, as long as you feel comfortable, people will gravitate to this so there is no need to be insecure, let that negative feeling go and release your inhibition. Work on your physical image to indicate positive change and maintain this standard, regardless of what people say it is your life and not theirs. We were all given one life to live so it is therefore ours to do as we wish!

Create sexy affirmations!

Create affirmations that spur you further in your endeavor, an amazing list is below!

Remember to mix them with feelings, belief and emotions for them to work!

I am beautiful inside and out.

I am interesting and sexy.

I have an adventurous spirit.

Men are naturally attracted to my radiant energy.

I am full of positive energy.

I am irresistible to men.

Men are drawn to my womanliness.

I light up a room.

Men are always noticing me.

I am a beautiful, confident, sexy woman.

I will attract great men into my life.

I am starting to feel more and more confident.

I am developing an attractive personality.

Men will be helpless to resist me.

My sexual energy is constantly growing and developing.

I will attract any man I want.

Men will be drawn to my energy.

I will develop my confidence.

Men are starting to approach me wherever I go.

My attitude is becoming more positive and attractive.

Feeling sexy and attractive is a normal part of my life.

Men are always pursuing me.

Men are naturally drawn to my wonderful personality.

I am tuned in to my sexual power.

Men love to be around me.

I naturally draw men to me in all situations.

I am just naturally confident and outgoing all the time.

Others see me as someone who always gets attention from men.

I can attract any man.

Men are naturally attracted to me.

You are a true goddess now. Follow through to the end, men will fall to your feet and worship you, you deserve it, you were meant to be happy. Life is meant to be fun and exciting, *not a bore . . .*

You are apart of an exciting generation of strong, independent and self-reliant women. *Embrace the change . . .*

Chapter 7:

The Magic of Sexual Energy

Let us now look into the untapped reserves of the sexual energy. Sex, if you did not know is a dance of energy. It is your contact with the vital forces of creation. It is also a declaration of your identity into this divine physical reality. Sexual expression is vital for vibrant health and well-being. Whenever it is blended with the emotion of love and the qualities of truthfulness and trust, it becomes your personal connection to the cosmos, wherein, portals open to the sacred mysteries of the universe.

Through sex expression you remind your body cells of your own vitality. The energy of sex is meant to keep you tuned into divine frequencies which is apart of what aids in the healing of your body.

The experience of orgasm directly connects you with spirit, it forms the bridge to the divine, and it reorganizes and revitalizes your body cells. During sex, hormones are released that alters your brain wave patters toward balance and integration, thus activating the awakened *cosmic* mind within you.

The power of an *orgasmic experience* can be a genital experience, a full-body experience or a multi-bodied, full-chakra opening, taking you on an amazing journey into the *multi-verse.*

A sexual experience is like a rocket booster. When coupled with *conscious intent*, it can propel you into aspects of reality that can enrich your mind, body and spirit, enriching your life and well-being.

When having sex, you are actually stirring the life-force kundalini energy located at the base of the spinal cord, in doing this, you are playing with powerful energy, with knowledge of it you are inviting this serpent like energy to come from its lair to teach you how to dance with life.

You have a responsibility to know and understand your own body and its vast ways in which it can be touched, played, stirred, positioned and stimulated to bring forth greater, breathtaking pleasures, and allow this energy to flow up your spine and spiral out through all realities.

In activating kundalini energy by means of sexual pleasure, you create direct openings into simultaneous dimensional experiences which have a direct interface with the life you are now living.

Love, Romance and Sex with a partner you are in love with is like rowing down a magical Nile in Egypt or traveling on a magic carpet to anywhere you desire.

Sexual energy is psychical energy and having sex with someone makes you literally take on that person's energetic field. Sexual energy embodies the power of creation and is therefore sacred and within your body, it is actually the most powerful and extraordinary source of energy you have to master.

In reading the above, you may have noticed you experienced a higher level of thought, good, come back and read this again several times. You have been exposed to *great magic*. Now that you are aware of how powerful sexual energy is, you should become aware that you can use it for whatever you desire, the key is your thoughts, being consciously aware of what you are doing or using it for.

Chapter 8:

The Ancient Art of Transmutation

This is the apex of this manual. Transmutation is in simple terms the changing or converting of one form of energy into another. During moments of sexual ecstasies, hold the thoughts or affirmations of becoming the greatest at oral sex, or hold the thought of your related affirmations and think about them intently, imagine the sexual energy that is being produced is being channeled into getting you what you want, in this case, propelling you into becoming greatest at oral sex, molding and reshaping you, and in doing this, you are performing an age old magic of *Alchemical Transmutation*. Keep this a secret, it is yours to keep and use as you desire. Remember, believing that this will work is the *spark* that lights the fire!

Chapter 9:

The Art of Oral Sex part 1:
Foreplay

The physical aspect of this philosophy begins with foreplay. Not all guys like foreplay but this part is for the ones who do and besides, you are now powerful being aware that you have power, you now have control over your sexual destiny and encounters, thinking he will like foreplay paves the way for it even if in the past he didn't, simply think it and believe it. Get some body oil and massage him down, even if you are terrible at it, never mind that, you are making him relax as your energy binds and casts its spell on him. You cannot see the forces at work, *you just have to believe.*

"You like when I touch you, I know you do," whisper this to him. In moments of him relaxing, his subconscious mind is becoming receptive towards suggestions and this is the goal, once you have him in this relaxed mode, you can cast countless spells on his mind with suggestions.

Get naked, strip down piece by piece. Let your very powerful feminine energy take hold of him. Let him see you in new bra and new panties; ignite that masculine flame inside him, that *flame* of *desire*.

"I love your cock inside me," nibble on his earlobe, let tingles flow down his spine.

"My pussy is wet for you . . ." say his name; bring out the demon in him that your power will tame!

"My pussy aches for you,"

"I want you inside me,"

When I whisper these seductive words, guys literally go crazy and rip my bra and panties off but let's take it slow. Remain in control ladies!

By now you are both feeling intense desires; the room is over pouring with it. Keep the temperature warm, let your sweats flow, its energy being burnt, imagine this energy being challenged inside you, making you great, making you sexy, making you more beautiful, making you powerful, imagine the energy binding him to you.

Kiss him gently. Hold the thought of you becoming the greatest at oral sex, when you become distracted and lost in the moment, snap back into it, remember it is your goal! Touch, squeeze, stroke, hold, hug and the like, keep it sensual girls and keep that energy flowing. Every contact sends chills coursing through his body!

Chapter 10:

The Art of Oral Sex
Part 2: The Act

Ask him repeatedly, let him beg you to, he wont mind you stalling him for its obvious from your look and dress that you have undergo changes so this change in your attitude is indeed expected, remember it's the first he is encountering with your new personality, the goddess.

"Tell me to suck your dick," whisper this seductively to him. Your voice will put him in a trance.

"Tell me, Tell me,"

"Tell me to suck it babe,"

"Do you like when I suck it?"

Sometimes guys gets annoyed with the line of chit chatting and wants action but remember, your aim goes beyond physical passion, you are performing magic so take your time girl.

Whisper to yourself in your mind before you begin.

I Am the greatest at oral sex.

He loves when I suck his dick.

I give him the best blow job.

He is addicted to me.

He finds me irresistible.

Hold these or related thoughts in your mind and feel energy and life going into these thoughts and affirmations. Do this and believe it.

Gently place the tip of his dick on your lip. Look into his eyes, from eye contact, energy is being transferred between you two. You being consciously aware of this puts you in control, using it gives you even more control. Cast yours spells.

It's also not a bad idea to give him a glass of wine or have one yourself, do not get drunk, remain fully conscious and aware but a glass of wine keeps me on fire. I like a cool glass of Chardonnay or Italian Moscato.

Feel the fire and passion, feel the desire. Your thoughts are on fire, your emotions ablaze and all this power is at your disposal, think about what you want and hold the thought of it.

I AM THE GREATEST AT ORAL SEX.

I AM THE GREATEST AT ORAL SEX.

I AM THE GREATEST AT ORAL SEX.

Place your tongue between his piss slit, your wet tongue massaging this sensitive spot sends waves of pleasures surging down his spinal cord from the base of his head. His insides are burning; he will glare at you with immense lust. Eye contact transfers energy between you two.

I AM THE GREATEST AT ORAL SEX.

I AM THE GREATEST AT ORAL SEX.

I AM THE GREATEST AT ORAL SEX.

Hold your thought.

Suck his dick slowly, your free hands should course up and down his leg if you are on your knees and if you are in bed, then softly pass your hand over his nipples and stomach. Take his entire dick into your mouth, gag, and make it wet and slippery.

I AM THE GREATEST AT ORAL SEX.

I AM THE GREATEST AT ORAL SEX.

I AM THE GREATEST AT ORAL SEX.

Hold the thought of your aim and believe energy is going into this and making it your reality.

He moans gently, yes, he is on fire for you . . .

Spit on his dick and suck it off. Alternate between fast, hard sucks and soft, slow, gentle ones.

I AM THE GREATEST AT ORAL SEX.

I AM THE GREATEST AT ORAL SEX.

I AM THE GREATEST AT ORAL SEX.

Repeat the thought into your mind. Suck him, blow his mind and know that a great power is at work for you!

Slap it on your lips, rub it on your lips, moan, it turns him on. His thoughts for you are filthy, blood surges through his veins, he is fully aroused and his dick is sensitive. The mood is set and the temperature is right, the energy feels right and you are harnessing it and using it.

Suck him faster and harder. *Imagine* him thinking that you are indeed the greatest at oral sex and their will be points when you will actually hear him moan that you are the greatest or the best, don't be shocked or think this is just coincidence, know that a power as old as time itself is at work for you, give thanks by saying "thank you for my infinite powers" and continue with your magic.

Occasionally look into his eyes and feel his energy . . .

I AM THE GREATEST AT ORAL SEX.

I AM THE GREATEST AT ORAL SEX.

I AM THE GREATEST AT ORAL SEX.

Hold your thought and persist.

You don't have to be an expert as yet, just hold your thought; a time will come when new techniques and styles for performing oral sex will just bolt into your mind out of nowhere and when you perform it, he will be swept away. *Just believe.*

When you proceed into sex. Hold your thoughts of what you want, look into his eyes while he is deep inside your wet pussy, in moments like these repeat what you want into your mind.

I AM THE GREATEST AT ORAL SEX.

I AM THE GREATEST AT ORAL SEX.

I AM THE GREATEST AT ORAL SEX.

Cry out in ecstasy and pain and know that a great power is working for you.

Only if you deeply believe this it will work, otherwise it won't. Believe it and failure will be impossible . . .

Chapter 11:

How to place a sexual spell on a guy

Do you want him to stick to you sexually? Or you wish for him to fall in love with you?

During sexual ecstasy, hold the thought of what you want, create the affirmation for it, write it down and constantly repeat it to yourself in a spirit of absolute faith.

Here are examples of affirmations you can use or edit.

(Insert his name here) You are in love with me and we are eternally happy.

(Insert his name here)) I am the love of your life and the center of your universe.

(Insert his name here) You love me eternally; I am the perfect match for you.

(Insert his name here) You are deeply in love with me, life is joyous and all is well.

(Insert his name here) I am your soul mate.

Chapter 12:

How to make him to stick to you sexually

Do you want him to stick to you sexually?

Then go ahead a step further and suggest sexual explicit affirmations to him while his mind is open and receptive during moments of high ecstasy.

Moan his name with what you desire and it will take deep roots into his mind and sprout the seeds of what you want, keep watering it and it will blossom and grow. See suggestions below!

(Insert his name here) You love fucking me, my pussy is right for you baby.

(Insert his name here) Fuck me, I love you, You cant stop fucking me.

(Insert his name here) My pussy loves when you fuck it baby, its yours baby, fuck it baby.

(Insert his name here) Your dick feels so good in me baby, it makes me so weak, I love it baby.

(Insert his name here) Oh, my pussy feels so good with you inside me baby, oh god.

(Insert his name here) Oh god baby, fuck me, you can't leave me baby, keep fucking me.

(Insert his name here) Don't leave me baby, I love how you fuck me baby.

He will respond by agreeing to everything you are saying or moaning in this case, these will sink into his mind, giving you the grip you will need.

These statements are powerful when you are consciously aware that you are taking your roots into this guys mind! Do not harbor doubt or fear into your mind, know with absolute faith that this works! Believe it the way Christians believe in the second coming of Christ! Whenever I say believe, this level of deep seated believe is what I am referring to, this deep magnitude of belief is what is required for your spells and magic to work. The human mind is fertile soil and thoughts we plant into it will grow seeds of its kind. Plant what you want into a guys mind and he is yours! Plant it and continue to nurture it!

Plant it at the height of ecstasy when either or both of you are coming and this electro-magnetic orgasmic force will put the icing on the cake and the plums in the plum pudding. Orgasm is powerful release of energy so take the golden opportunity of affirming what you want during moments of it and it works wonders for you!

This is the greatest spell of spells!
Rise Ladies!

Read this book over and over and over again and put the practice into action, begin your transformation, begin your rebirth, free yourself of the chains that bound you and unleash your feminine energy and use it for whatever you desire, whenever you desire.

Share the magic by telling a friend about it, there is something in this book for everyone . . .

Thank you so much for reading.

THANK YOU SO MUCH FOR READING!

PLEASE REMEMBER TO LEAVE ME YOUR *CUSTOMER REVIEWS*, LOOKING TOWARDS READING THEM ALL!

7051443R00036

Printed in Germany
by Amazon Distribution
GmbH, Leipzig